only time

poems by marcia jones

ISBN 978-1-949053-07-4

Pinecone Book Company
P.O. Box 65 | Evergreen, Colorado 80437
PineconeBookCo@gmail.com

In memory of Melvin Rosen, my father.
You had the heart of a poet.

For Carolyn Evans Campbell, my poetry teacher and friend.
You inspire me.

Contents

time to let go   127

With Appreciation   149

From the Poet   150

Our existence is but a brief crack of light
between two eternities of darkness.
Vladimir Nabokov

only time

To everything there is a season,
and a time to every purpose under heaven.
Ecclesiastes 3:1

I Sing

Inspired by Walt Whitman's Song of Myself

I sing of myself
I sing of America
I sing of being born a woman
I sing when I fly

I sing when I fly
over black oak branches in apricot-flushed sky
over birds erupting like ink splashed from my inkwell
over immigrant ships westbound
on rippled bronze glass

over war fought between brothers
and war between strangers

I fly over spent pioneers bent to tame rough land
over explorers in canoes at forks of gashing rivers
over plains heaving with the hot breath of buffalo

over ragged hungry survivors
on barren water-rushed shores
over my Belgian grandmother pulling spring onions
her long skirt swinging

over schoolgirls dreaming of futures without horizons

I touch my mother's water-flushed womb
I see lightning slice the continental divide
I see a candle light a young girl's path to wisdom
I sing of war nurses packing worn satchels for killing fields
I hear slave mothers torn from babies

I see all that is light
I see all that is dark
all that shames
and all that transcends

My spirit is American
and it flows from me

I sing of myself
and I sing of you

I touch miners trapped in black cages
I see dust bowl mothers scrounge scraps
so empty children eat and someday smile

I feel heat from first votes of 20th century women
and from Abigail Adams scratching an eagle feather quill
from her century to mine

I see prairie teachers bending to stoves in winter
I follow Rosa Parks to the front of the bus

I cry with grandpapa as he lies in his garden
attacking weeds with his cutoff hoe
with Rose as she leaves Irish starvation
to work indentured in the house of a stranger
and with great-great grandfather who loved her

I wake to dawn's amethyst dew
and lift my face to slashed rain
I smell each fresh leaf on every tree and it is mine
I hold all children at Sandy Hook and they are mine

I smell lilacs in the dooryard as last they bloom
I soar above Benjamin Franklin's first shared library

I escape into old farmhouses with worn wood floors
and listen to the night symphonies of crickets

I remember underground railroads
where old quilts signaled the way of hope
I hear the voice of our first woman president
I wonder at the moon landing
I dream in the static of stars
I weep at the fine words of Thomas Jefferson

I swoop to touch wild prairie grass
and listen to the music of flutes brought from home
in a covered wagon crossing the plains

I dream of the legacy of Eleanor Roosevelt
and reach for the strains of *Rhapsody in Blue*
I peer through orange-crimson leaves
into grey barns and onto blue shores of the great lakes
I stalk a red fox under sharp white stars

I watch a veiled young widow walk beside a coffin

I hear robins break through soft aqua shells
see my mother believe in moonrise as she lay dying

I feel the rage of western wildfires
the passion of Martin Luther King's blaze of freedom
the hypocrisy of white-hooded violators
I feel the crash burn of 19th century electricity
see women in coveralls rivet for the war
hear women sing and thrive with new freedom

I touch ginger ember feathers of the red-tailed hawk
and weep with the slaughter in a city of parks
I smell flood waters rising in New Orleans

I touch magpies grooming the backs of does
I hear Abraham Lincoln's timeless speech at Gettysburg
I feel death's shadow stalking in Vietnam

I am a speck in the universe
I am one
I am all
I am a columbine thriving strong
among millions of granite years

John Steinbeck writes a masterpiece
in the golden hills of the west
Walt Whitman sings a song of himself
and of all America

I fly past eons of my future
bending back to my past

I sing
I fly

I feel longing in everyone

After the Storm

The air is fresh with torn greenness.
Chartreuse leaves, tender,
just sprung, slice from aspens
that scrape the wounded blue-black sky.
Green spears rip from wind-hurled pines
to collide with blue needles and fragile twigs.

A still afternoon is battered
with breakers of hail, reminding me
of moments when life is calm,
in balance, and a single crack
with no warning, maybe once
in a lifetime, upends everything.

Nothing is the same after the storm.

Slowly Spinning in Yellow

A delicate begonia
broken at the neck
falls from a pot of dazzling
yellow orange and red.

I chase a poem and slide
down an orange-red petal
into gentle yellow, a womb
silky as a tropical bird's breast.

I luxuriate in the glow
of those sun-warm walls
shaded with red petals
and edged with wilted black lace.

Like a slow-danced tango
my poem ignites with splendor,
and I linger inside that red begonia,
slowly spinning in yellow.

Dust of Forever

In a cyclone of fierce grief, trapped
between low sky and hard earth,
she aches for freedom she once owned.

She rips earth's soil, seeking the core
of her sorrow. When she finds it,
she knows she can live with it.

She tears the night sky, sloughing stars,
slinging blackness, searching for a way
to heal—to connect.

She sees her grief—she is alone.
She sees grief in everyone—she is not alone.
She is not alone in the dust of forever.

Where Only We Have Been

I have my father's hands
hands that held me
on the night I dreamed a tiger
hands that sheltered me
in the crash of rain

hands that tossed me
laughing into the air
and always caught me
coming down

aged hands
hands that explored my face
to work out who I was

our hands are a geography
of cracked earth
ancient riverbeds
purple hills ravaged
with sun and drought
a geography where only we have been

No End in Sight

The universe pounds
mystery, restlessness.
We are one flute crying
in a wild symphony.

In the vast unimaginable
we are specks, yet the universe
sings in our darkness,
and we fly through galaxies

on holiday from Earth, leaving
behind unrest and greed,
and although we relentlessly seek,
there is no end in sight.

That Moon-Washed Night

You lay dying,
bathed in blue moonlight sifting
through your open bedroom window
from a mother-of-pearl September sky
washed with fragrant summer-late air—
three of us as one—you, I, and the moon.

You knew it would be your last night,
your face, alabaster pale, chiseled,
every fragile bone a reminiscence
of where you'd been, your head
smooth, proud, letting me know
in your final loss, you were undefeated.

You whispered, no regrets,
you could have spilled over with regrets,
instead your path opened to forgiveness
for others and for yourself, a resolute pilgrim
wrapped with warm light in a shroud
of moon sheen.

Imagine

You twist your kaleidoscope
to the unknown. Anticipation
shocks like a doe leaping through
silver leaves in a summer wood.

Your time is waning,
your years unleashed.
You understand mysteries
more clearly than answers.

Time is capricious, freewheeling,
and in your kaleidoscope
dreams collide with desire,
yearning, and most of all, chance.

Blue Hour

I walk alone into the mountain.
I walk into myself. I let go
of my yearning, my song melts
in alpenglow.

The mountain beckons,
my timeless friend.
Wind-wounded trees
bend to light, surrender to silence.

You could have come with me,
but I lean to the mountain
alone, not lost.
My ashes drift to dust.

I hold the arm of night's wind
and reach to stars,
hot in my blue hour.
I cry because I have climbed.

I have climbed
this eternal mountain
in its blue-clear
mystery.

three haiku

just one shy sly glance
before you sigh behind clouds
love at first moon sight

    arranged on a hill
    dark notes in a requiem
    bison graze and sing

        such a sharp morning
        light so white it stings and laughs
        after night's mourning

Until the Night

No night is so opaque
that you can't find a star
if you wander far enough.
By morning you are grounded,
steady, with just a smirk of knowing
you have been to your dark
and back again. Now you know
you will always make it home,
until the night you won't.

Moonwalk

It's two in the morning,
and the hail just stopped cold.
I open my door to an ice-pure moonscape.
Glistening. Chilling.

My boot prints plait with your paw prints,
and we melt a moon-path in ice pebbles.
We wander across slight hills, slender rills
into an eerie wilderness, unsettling,
for above us another moon,
an eloquent crescent,
wanes and winks
as she prepares to sleep.

Starshine

Together, you and he
held all of life.
Now you hold
memories of touching,
loving, laughing.

Darkness softens
in a tender dawn
heavy with longing,
but your story
lingers

until night's last
pale stars bow
then slow dance
into starshine,
into morning.

Girls' Night Out

In this morning's wee hours,
you and I slip and slide
through amethyst-striped
spring snow.

A half-moon eyes us
suspiciously from the west,
her ancient parchment face
half-washed in ivory light
through night's ice mist.

An awareness as delicate
and stirring as quickened
beatings of our hearts, and a doe
rises from frost fog that cloaks
two silver yearlings.

Not moving, they watch us
in stone-silence from across
a slender frozen creek.

Last Things

Extravagant, elegant, a meteor shower
splinters the sky, stings the Earth
with dancing light, then swoops
in blackness to eternity.

Bundled in blankets I lie on wet grass,
tingle with the delicate fingers of dread.
The time is coming for last things.
Last summer. Last star. Last breath.

dream theatre

sigh me to sleep, lift me
from my sleep-storm
into the crisp unknown
of nightness, fly with me
from the cage of my bed,
excite me, raise night's curtain
to abandoned stories,
ignite my dream stage
with restless illusions
of tousled lovers,
and capture delusions
that sizzle by my bed
until morning explodes
like birds let go in the light

only time

she lifts her face to the night
she breathes with the wind
she challenges the universe
and reaches for its cruel riddle
of time

only time

she knows better
than to ask for more time
everyone wants more of it

everyone is born with it
at first heartbeat

everyone loses it
with each heartbeat

I look up
and even though
I know better I ask
I ask for more time

only time

once upon a time

Every past used to be a future
once upon a time.
Munia Khan

Northern Light

*Inspired by my great-grandmother, who emigrated
from Sweden in the late nineteenth century*

Secret dreamer
you paced
an immigrant ship's deck
and created a story
that will never end.

Wearing old shoes made of wood
and beat up leather, you longed
for white satin shoes
soft as fawn spots
clean, and small, and new.

You carried an old butter press
and a pair of silver Swedish sleigh bells
baked in a loaf of black bread
made with alder tree dust
and old rye flour.

You remembered
the mud and dung of cow stalls
left behind
when you, the morning milkmaid,
brought forth fresh milk and cream.

Your feet propped up
on the cows' sides
your skirts arced wide above your ankles
you dreamed an unfinished poem
or hummed an arctic song.

You turned
from bittersweet roots
in hard-rocked fields
to untie your tangled bramble-hair
and dance unbound in new America.

Now and then, you weep
with dark memories
of bleak winter solstices,
yet your Nordic eyes
reflect millennia of aurora borealis.

Your pioneer soul
ignites your path with swaths
of radiant light,
purple crimson pink
violet blue.

Who are you?
You, who carried
legends and mysteries
from your world to mine?
Tell me your secrets.

She Was Born to March

She was born with the mystery of the St. Joseph River
under a sulky grey sky, mile upon mile of river
flowing alive like the blood in her veins,
finally rolling to an icy collision with the great lake.

She was born in anticipation of early flowers,
wild, growing amok along the mighty river
on the floor of dark northern woods,
fragrant with Winter's leftover rot.

She was born when Winter overstayed his visit,
and Spring dropped in without an invitation,
wet-drunk, ready to pound earth into its ancient scent.
She was born to March. And March was born to her.

Perfection

In the late fifties, not quite a teen,
you sit for a formal photograph
in an Olan Mills Studio, second floor
of a dreary Sears & Roebuck's.
In front of a black curtain, you
hope for a likeness that looks
a little less like you than you.

Your new turquoise sateen dress
caresses you up and down.
It's your first grown-up dress,
pencil-straight and sleek.

Your hair bends, a perfect bubble bob.
Your lips pout with just-back-in-style
Revlon's Gentlemen Prefer Red.

The photographer is poised for action.
*All right. Sit straight, turn your head
slightly to the left, no more to the right,
lower your eyes, now just a hint of a smile,
oh, too much, shift your shoulders forward
just a bit, not too far, move back just a hair,
chin up a little, tilt to the right...say cheese!*

Arranged to someone else's perfection,
you are now a complete fake.

Coming of Age

Best friends for life,
we worked our high school job
that November afternoon
balancing profit and loss,
red and black,
while we listened to Clair de Lune
on the radio until shocking news
disrupted the ticking of our calculators.

John F. Kennedy. Dead.

We fled into afternoon light
under clouds rushing like white cranes
against autumn sky, cold enough
to see each other's breaths,
our silence shattered only by dead leaves,
blood red and crunched under foot.

We had only just heard, but already
the news felt like a memory, a letting go
of what had been, and a letting go
of what was to come.

I pushed you hard into a pile of leaves,
your blazing hair tangled
in lifeless maple and oak.
No laughing now.
You stood up and shoved me
hard into another mound.

birds on a line

To my adventurous poet friends: Kay, Peggy, Barrie, Kari, and Janie

sizzling June sky invites zippers to zip
poet-chicks chuckle chit chit chatty chip
six mountain birdies are ready to flip

first to take off, magpie eager to tease
seeking someone to pester, someone to seize
a chatterbox floating high on the breeze

second to leap, spring robin red breast
she's ready to soar, fresh from her nest
an expert zipper, always the best

third to zip off, dove, fruffled and fine
cooing, who-whooing, pine to pine
all of a sudden, she lets go of the line

fourth to leap, petite hummingbird
fuchsia lime red smack yellow, whirred
her wings on fire, smoking, blurred

last on the line, gull, eager to flee
white flames, she flies, wings in a V
swooping, diving, open and free

beware an imposter, jay, stellar and sly
at the finish line she sneak-sings a lie
pretending she'd zipped all day, oh my!

Eyeshine

I slammed you,
a lanky nocturnal hunter,
miles from home
on an untamed night
under gauzy moon-clouds
casting night shadows
of dappled coyotes dancing
on an eternal highway,
my solitary journey
lighted only with headlights,
a high fuzzy moon,
and a star or two in the north.

Heading west, windows open,
now and then a distant howling
behind willful black mountains
above sagebrush etched silver
on an endless-to-nowhere horizon,
I broke you.

In one lightning second,
you, pale phantom,
streaked through my lights.
I spoiled you.

The violence of it stopped us,
you limped low into indifferent
brush, glancing back
for one ephemeral moment,
your gold-green eyeshine
piercing mine.

Or, did I, in that timeless flash,
see only my eyes
shining back at me?

Secret Art Show

Close your eyes and enter a secret art show.
Behind your eyelids float hallucinations,
gold hoops, and neon orange stripes
on a plush black canvas with scorched images
from the last scene you glimpsed.
Squeeze your eyes to violet sunbursts
on a silver screen, red chrysanthemums
on gold satin.

No one will see this show but you.

I Was Formed by

I was formed by storms,
black, wind-torn storms from the lake,
mid-western storms from the mid-century.

I was formed by a handsome, gentle-strong
father and a beautiful fragile-strong
mother who loved each other
until they couldn't.

I was formed by compromise
the eighth summer Daddy left,
my collection of Mama's tears,
their bitter fight over two shaken girls,
and the foreboding of a blended family tree,
scarred with grafts that never took.

Judges

Fat black crows glisten with rain,
huddle under downcast trees,
waddle like pious Victorian clerics,
billowing robes open to the wind.

A congregation of magpies scold,
criticize, grab attention.

Finally, having had enough,
the crows lift their black arms
to pass judgment from bare branches
on high.

Stained Shadows

A faraway god
ruled from his gold throne,
tsk-tsking me in my innocence,
following and judging me
through silver Bible clouds.

A devil
hid under my bed,
keeping me awake
with his blazing pitchfork
and come-hither sneer.

Pious pews
held me straight and stifled
washed in purple shadows
and blood-red stained glass,
my hands clenched

in spotless white gloves
beneath my small white smile
while I questioned it all.
Whispers rustled among the faithful
that I might end up a nonbeliever.

How could that be
when I believed in so much—
the Earth,
fierce shooting stars,
and the radiance of poems?

Wardrobe Malfunction

Oops, we have no spacesuit
in your size. Smash your dream
of the first female-team spacewalk.

We men walked on the moon,
planted rovers on Mars, drifted
all over space in suits perfectly
fitted to our manly physiques.

Never once did we think
to create a space wardrobe
for you – and so soon.

After all, it was only a century ago
that we allowed you to vote.
And maybe a half century ago
that, grudgingly, we allowed you
to take our jobs, become CEOs
and astronauts, and earn 80 cents
on the dollar.

And look how that turned out.

Remember

I walked through the cemetery today.

When did Memorial Day slip into a holiday
merely to mark summer's start? Summer solstice
shines in June. To the thoughtless it is a day
off work to camp, lie on the beach, dance.

I walked through the cemetery today with flowers
for my grandfather's grave. The groundskeeper
told me deer eat all the real flowers.
I said, whatever, deer must eat too.

I will never bring gaudy plastic flowers
to honor my loved ones, only vibrant flowers
of summer.

I walked through the cemetery today,
thought how beautiful it looks.
Flags rose from graves of the fallen
all the way to the horizon.

The cemetery wept with ancient symbolism,
wrapped me in peace. I remembered.

I walked through the cemetery today.

The Real Deal

Your email is a kiss through a screen door,
welcome, tender, and more exciting
than no kiss at all, cool and quick.

But your letter, in messy script,
is a real-deal kiss, a wide open door,
sending shocks right through me.

Den of Iniquity

A memory seared
into my coming of age years
when I peeked into
his forbidden room.

His basement man cave,
outlawed to little girls,
but with a pull so great
I dreamed of sneaking in.

Finally, when the coast was clear,
I crept down the stairs
and cracked open the door.
I would need time to take it all in!

I was a girl raised
in the *Straight and Narrow*,
and this was a foreign land.
It felt like sin city!

Knotty pine walls
heavy with deer trophies
and calendars with
nearly naked women!

A rustic bar stretching
from wall to wall
with an endless row
of red leather bar stools.

An entire back wall
lined with amber liquors,
with flamboyant labels
of red, gold, silver, and black.

Card tables strewn
with chips, dirty glasses,
Pabst Blue Ribbon bottles,
half-chewed cigars.

And everywhere the acrid scent
of last night's cigarettes and spilled beer.
A den of iniquity,
my father would have said.

Ruthless in Red

My ruthless pen
obsessed editing queen
svelte in your red pencil dress.
Your silver stilettoes
slash the passive voice
hack subject-verb disagreements
slice misplaced apostrophes
and wild commas.
Finally, after slaying
clichés and redundancies
you toss their parts in your bin
and click click click away
without a backward look.

When You Remember

When you remember
coarse white sheets
bucking in winter's wind
and first hard snow,
frozen like icy boards,
pinned on the line, pure
and fresh as winter's breath

When you remember
slipping into bed on those
clean stiff sheets, cold,
bearing afternoon's air,
a faded red-hot water bottle
at your feet softening
the fierce chill

When you remember
all the winters racing
from the lake, the untimely
darkness, the tree ghost-limbs
looming angry at your window,
your sheets rough
to your face

Then you remember
your winter story
where gnawing winds
and low skies
made you strong
in the face of anything anywhere

time and chance

I'll sit and see if that small sailing cloud
will hit or miss the moon. It hit the moon.
Robert Frost

first love

we lay hot,
hidden all day
in sandy cleavages
of dunes
under heavy wet air
and essence
of Coppertone,
sweat, longing,
taking chances
on first love

Today's Miracle

Two hours of flurry for us,
Two hours of terror for a tiny bird.
We almost trip on him, a fragile hummer,
more delicate than fine blown glass.
He lies silent on his back in our hot garden,
downcast in relentless July sun,
his iridescent miniature feathers on fire,
cobalt raspberry emerald green gold.

Gently we slip his frail body, weighing
less than a penny, onto a dustpan,
lay him in aspen shade on cool grass.

Maybe his wing is broken, snagged as it is
on his delicate twig leg. He pants,
tries to rise, valiant, determined, afraid.

We offer sugar water in an eye dropper,
his tiny sliver-tongue laps life-juice.
Is he suffering? We squeeze more juice
until he stops drinking to eye us as if to say
thank you, my friends. He wears down,
kaleidoscope breast glistening. He grasps,
gasps for breath. He can't stand up.

Mother Nature will decide his fate.

Later, we steal back
to peek at his resting place,
we hear almost-silent rustling in the grass,
then thep-thep   thep-thep-thep   thep-thep,
one flash, and he flies!

Nameless

You never told me your story.

You stood next to me at an assembly line,
my summer job in the heat of the late sixties.

All the world over so easy to see
people everywhere just wanna be free...

Your concentration camp number
glared angry and black on your thin arm.

Your dark Baltic eyes held unspeakable secrets.
You haunted me then. I didn't reach out.

Now, a half century later,
I don't even remember your name.

spring rage

mother of aspens
at the mercy of spring rain
you snap and are still

trio of proud trunks
cracked in night's fog-storm
you lie defeated

mother nature breaks
your life in her spring whim
to end your long reign

Drama Queen

Colorado you are a drama queen
wearing your heart on your sleeve

you flirt with untamed abandon
it's all about you

your mood swings from spring
to autumn in one summer day

you throw a tantrum then tease
with an upside-down smile

you are seductive, capricious,
and radiant with mystery

wild rainbow, you keep me wondering
and that is why I will never leave you

the answer

the answer
is blowin' in the wind

stained glass windows shine
in grand cathedrals,
and we ask why this extravagance
when so many children are hungry

incivility and inaction of politicians
fester under the Capitol dome,
and we ask when Americans
will put country over party

pale dust over distant mountains
rises from the void of war,
and we ask why killing never stops
in ancient lands

millions of women hammer
small cracks in the highest glass ceiling,
and we ask why it has taken centuries
to shatter and fall

the bronze Lady Liberty
lights her torch of American freedom,
and we ask why so many people
are still yearning to be free

the answer
is blowin' in the wind

Odds

You
faceless specter, stoke me
with untamed ice-fingers
and snatch me from millions.
Who are you? What do you want?
My name is Death you sneer.
I stalk before I kill...

She
meets me for lethal cocktails,
strangers tethered by tubes,
slow-drunk on a drip drip drip
of dark hope, anticipating hard
detours in our journey, hoping odds
aren't against us, until...

I
sigh with hope of survival
in wildflower dreams. Petals,
blue and orange, soothe me
like trembling butterfly wings,
and soft wash me in coolness
and healing, silent, so still...

Wheel of Fortune

Half a weary century ago
she spun the wheel of fortune
to win solitary confinement
and Jesus. Now she broods
in white silence in her black habit
of ferocious obedience, yearning
and lonely, wondering when
she went bankrupt, steeling herself
for a dreamless night, dreading
the blush of another day.

Celestial Coincidence

Dark luminescence wanes waxes
on a celestial path radiant as burnished brass.
A high-sky dream hushes, then hastens songbirds
impatient for new light.

Almost a century we waited for this eclipse,
not knowing what would be unleashed
as we walked into the mysterious and the infinite,
longing for something greater than ourselves.

Almost a century held desire, despair, and chance.
Now on this fierce summer morning,
we look skyward as our Earth, moon, and burnt sun
collide across our wounded country,

a country breaking with unrest,
afraid to love or let go,
and for two minutes we trust the universe.
We look up, we unite in celestial coincidence.

upside-down moon

peaceful
    upside-down
        blue moon

you caress me
with feather-shadow light
float me in fly-by-night calm

intrepid
    upside-down
        harvest moon

you shatter me
with no warning
splinter my night with orange-fire knives

impetuous
    upside-down
        blood moon

you tempt me
with fate in your cinder-eye
possess me forever in your restless heart

Salvador

These days he carries a few shirts,
rusty pans, and bedraggled books
in a pack on his back. He sleeps
where he can under rain, sun, wind
on his *unlucky* days.

Sometimes he crashes in an old tent
in someone's overgrown back yard.
Desolate even on his *lucky* days.

He bends to ruthless soil
at wealthy homes, sweltering
in southern California's white sun
for a few dollars on his *very lucky* days.

He drips sweat as he waters, trims,
rakes, weeds, hoes, digs, plants.
He caresses his trees, shrubs, flowers,
and tells them of the cool comfort
of old poems, of cherished words
that take him almost home.

His name is Salvador.
Savior.

Dread

Spring crept in on April Fools' Day,
but winter's dread fought its momentum.
Fear is back, a flood flashing
down an unsuspecting canyon,
destroying summer dreams.

suspense

one fickle droplet
suspends
tense electric
trembling
from a silver
icicle
a cold-gashed
water light
lengthens
like a liquid
exclamation point
then either
freezes
a cruel stiletto
or sighs
and plunges
with eloquent
release

They Could Be Anywhere

Today's scan does not show
rogue cells, my doctor proclaims
no evidence of disease.

Hey doc—wait! Have you looked
everywhere—head to toe, high and low,
to and fro?

Could those double-crossing
con artists still lurk somewhere
in my thirty-seven trillion cells?

They've pulled this trick before.
Are they sneering and leering
from their dark hidey-holes?

Memories Like Paper Lanterns

Love forever exists in the soul-lit space of memory. —*Angie Wieland-Crosby*

Memories, ephemeral, shimmer like light-fired paper lanterns,
almost out of reach, always on the edge of disappearing.

Her *now* spirals to her *before* and she remembers.
Fragile memories float, shimmer, slow burn in her dreams.

She glimpses maelstroms in centuries of soul-lit memories,
all before she became…

Before she erupted with force from the shore beam
of her mother's womb, stunned in the surprise of light.

Before she sang in the womb, longing to linger warm
forever in its sea, its tide whispering in out in out.

Before she swam in stillness, her rope tied, tangled,
anchored with her mother's spirit, entwined, alive.

Before she touched her mother's cry at her conception.

Inspired by Memories Like Paper Lanterns, mixed media, Lynn Allbright

River of No Return

You don't have to keep them… you just point them back across the river and let them swim for it. —Ken Cuccinelli, Immigration Services

Papá, this morning you whispered, we're going to swim it.
Conquer it. Drink it. This barrier everyone calls the rough
river will never haunt us again.

Week upon week we walked, two thousand miles of dust,
escaping southern violence and despair to meet the heat,
white-furious, of *El Norte's* promise of asylum.

Week upon desperate week we waited, seared by brutal sun
and hunger, for our turn to cross the river.
Thugs on the bridge make sure we don't cross
unless we pay. Today, as yesterday, we have no money.

Now you say we won't wait any longer. We'll wade
into the cool danger of this grand river and swim
to the unknown.

Under our blue and red shirts, hope beats hot and hard.
You whisper that this crossing is for me, your little dreamer.

I climb on your back, crawl under your shirt and hang on.
I am safe with you, and *mamá* is right behind us.
Aloof water rouses us. We won't stop now,
for this river frightens us no more than the land we fled.

Swim, *papá*!

Fickle water, impulsive water captures us.
You fight restless currents until, among tangled nests
of slender reeds in pale water, we sink to cool mud
in our new land.

Papá, where's *mamá*? We lost her! Go back!
Go back without me! No, *papá*! No! Come back!
I'm afraid on this side. Don't leave me, *papá*,

I'm coming with you!

Tucked again into the sanctuary of your soaked shirt,
grasping your shoulders slick with river water,
we buck tangled currents back to *mamá*.

The river is crueler this time. Cold-hearted. Relentless.
You gasp, there's no talking now. Your strong arms flail.
You yell that you must save me first, your little angel.

This river wants to swallow us, *mamá*!
Struggling back toward the southern shore and *mamá*,
you wrestle with the river as we are dashed downstream,
farther, farther from our American Dream.

Fight *papá*! Breathe! Pray! Don't let go!

Papá!

Oh, god of the border, are you listening? We are all praying.
Hear us, hear us. We're too close to be this far away.

No one hears us.

Troubled water throws us to rocks, unforgiving.
Our blood dyes the river the red of unspeakable wrong.
Tense white currents heave us, not to the home
we imagined, but to an almost-home of another name.

You are fading blue, *papá*. I fight to hold on.
You fight to breathe.

I feel you surrender silently to the shallows, the mud,
the writhing reeds so far from *mamá*,
who still watches upstream on the southern shore.

I remember how much I love to dance and sing,
but we are trapped. You're fading blue, *papá*.
I can't feel you breathe. We're slipping into darkness.

We no longer see the other side. *El Norte*.

Lie beside me, *papá*. Lie beside me
in this June-warm shore-water. Rest, rest
at last under this merciless white sky.

We are seized, seized by this river wall.
We are stopped, stopped from our dream.

We are silenced, silenced in the white lies
we told ourselves and each other
at this grand river of no return.

as time goes by

I want to be light and frolicsome.
I want to be improbable beautiful
and afraid of nothing
as though I had wings.
Mary Oliver

October Regret

Nothing gold can stay. —Robert Frost

Today the continental divide
glows white light, white light
in a watercolor, transparent
under blue-sky brilliance.
It stabs my eyes—alive-fresh
first snow brushed on aspen
that only days ago set hills afire,
now ashen from first winter winds.
It's the first time I've missed
my journey up and over Squaw Pass
to wade in tides of Indian yellow,
my spirit time, my last lone day trip.
Now, nothing seems more important
than never again to miss
my last unbound journey
before winter.

High Coo

oowoo-woo-woo-woo
woeful cry from high coo nest
new life—dawn's promise

Anticipation

I was dreaming
about the design
and décor of my nest,
about each artfully
placed twig,
a neutral palette
with soft grey lint,
a bit of accent
mud, perhaps a berry
for a pop of color,
rustic yet elegant,
contemporary yet homey...

Oh no!
Another construction delay,
a foot of snow and counting...
no problem.

While I wait,
I'll hang out in spring leaves,
green crystal, and sing.

Sacred Secrets

The eastern sky glows the color
of my grandmother's hair, pale grey-blue, cold.

A perfect moon soft-shines,
a nineteenth century streetlamp in the first snow.

Why is the moon so mysterious?
Brave men have walked its pure terrain.

Still, each night, drenched in cloud light,
it hints to me of sacred secrets.

Night Reader

In the end, we'll all become stories.   —Margaret Atwood

In her blushing-pink bedroom,
a girl burns, blurs into a woman.
Scarred bookcases hold everlasting words,
unread, unexplored.

Every night rows of books beckon, rouse,
comfort her, and she can't wait to open them
in the same way she aches to grow up,
only imagining the thrill of discovery,

Allure
freedom
adventure
no turning back.

Every night
she reads
she rises
she escapes.

She escapes from her innocent bed
with Jo's dreams and fearless spirit,
with Scarlett's spunk in a flaming city,
with Eliza's courage on rafts of ice.

Riders on the Earth

To see Earth as it truly is, small and blue
and beautiful in that eternal silence as it floats,
is to see ourselves as riders on the Earth...
—Archibald MacLeish

From far away, the Earth,
a dot of life, sails blue white blue white
in a black sea, an arc of light.

I part the sea's black silk, cool,
luxurious, deep. The Earth beckons.
I drift from myself. I see.

I see one people. No right-left.
No sides of aisles, no me first. No war.
No one percent, no walls.

I see people more alike than unalike.
They look skyward from an open range
vast enough for all riders on the Earth.

One-Day-at-a-Time Day Tripper

January wind rages raw-edged,
throws her against hard snow.
Alone, she braces for forces
that fling old fears, not forgotten,
across her anxious landscape.

Storms spark bygone pain
that now and then
still burn razor white.

Gusts scrub grit
from the year's untidy start
when she, a *one-day-at-a-time day tripper*,
wondered if she would make it home
before dark.

Everywoman

You ignited revolution
Susan B. Anthony,
you expanded our potential
you always could foresee.

You're a great heroine, I will
sing your glorious song,
you devoted your fierce life to
put right a painful wrong.

Failure is impossible, you
cried as you fought to vote,
you were ridiculed, ostracized
but still you spoke, you wrote.

Women's options were so narrow
we *always* knew our place,
but your wages offered freedom,
thus your alligator case!

That smart case became your symbol
free from centuries of denial,
it carried speeches, pamphlets,
and a transcript of your trial.

It also held bold dreams of votes,
of equal work and pay,
of woman's suffrage catching fire
to light our path today.

One century after you were born
sweet victory at last,
when every woman could rejoice
Nineteenth Amendment passed!

on the hill

flashes of black and white,
a magpie caucus screeches
truth, or lies, from deep inside
a busy pine tree

glossy aubergine wings flail,
a conference of crows cries
truth, or lies, from atop
a nearby roof

there they go again,
they keep their distance,
squabble left and right,
truth and lie—cacophony

they jar us, cry fake news,
claim truth to power,
shriek *me me me*, fight high
here on the hill

No Horizons

For Julie and Harry's wedding. —inspired by Rumi

Forever love and we fly.
We imagine. We know.
We breathe. We dream. We cry.

Before our love we were silent,
cocooned, seeking love's language,
longing for flight.

Now, no longer resisting
the call of something stronger
than mere words can describe,

love lifts us,
each from our chrysalis,
on wings eager with desire

we enter today a sacred place
where only lovers meet to hold horizons
of each other's pounding heart.

From here we see only time.
Time to love, to grow, to wonder.
Time to console, to trust, to share

until death do us part.
We fly with no horizons
like brilliant butterflies toward home.

Invisible

The bad news…
You are falling from top
to bottom, plunging south,
drooping, dithering.

Once-lush hair, now overcast,
no longer flirts or sparks
in sunlight.

Your face, your memoir,
reflects each laugh, each grief
in your inimitable story.

Seasoned hands reveal sunspots,
callouses, blue rivulet veins,
reminders of a vital life.

The good news…
No one looks at you anymore.
No leers, no catcalls,
no ratings from one to ten.

You are invisible, a woman,
blissfully at peace
with herself.

Tip of the Iceberg

Lonely aqua spire, cold and icy fire,
looms lustrous, jagged, reaches for the moon,
reflected turquoise lights a sea of sapphire.

Silent apparition rises higher,
sings a desolate, haunting tune,
an eternal ghostly Arctic crier.

Pretty Pied Piper

Pretty Pied Piper, smashing
in your dashing yellow, grey,
white down jacket.

Silken feathers, white ruffles
spread wide in welcome
when I call your name.

Head nested, beak buried
in the collar of your elegant
feather-vest, at home with me.

Scorching orange-sweet cheeks
like the rouged disc of the sun
setting on a summer day.

Black eyes, dots gleaming in your
cocked head, ready to wink
while we gossip in tiny voices.

One slender foot tucked in the hem
of your shirt. You sleep now,
fluffed, peaceful as a summer cloud.

transition

cottonwoods bend low
rustle in ghostly wind
brave copper leaves hitch a ride
from November into winter

ten ways with words

i
hurl painful words
against the wall until they break,
then sweep them into street gutters

ii
fill your arms with words, serif fonts
that scratch your skin like kindling
ready to be ignited

iii
gather all the words you threw
in anger or you will discover
you can never get them back

iv
plant letters, nourish them,
grow them into words,
reap them for your masterpiece

v
let delicate letters sing
in artistic script on notes of light
inside your story

vi
catch a downpour of black letters
in your upside-down umbrella,
and rescue a drenched poem

vii
never mistreat words
or abbreviate life
in 140 tweet characters

viii
rip *sort of, you know, um,* and *like*
from sentences, crinkle them,
toss them into your bin

ix
remember words trigger actions,
and those actions can speak
louder than words, but not always

x
beware of feral words snarled
like ravens flying wild from winter trees
ajdko!ep1 brk!&mkmk3j!@ #2847jfk!*

My Protector

It's a whirlwind day, a yellow-spring day.
It's a mountain-mad day.

Your barking beckons me
quick-hurry to our glass door.

It's not your gruff bark
or your slow drawl bark
or your upbeat social bark.

This time, it's your warning bark.

On the hillside,
it's not a rabid lion,
it's not a suspicious boogeyman,
it's not a postal carrier.

It's a flimsy white shopping bag
somersaulting
over new grass,
a frantic plastic bird.

Your vigilance overwhelms me.
You save me from the wanton plastic bag
now snagged in a pine tree.

Relieved, you are your old self,
my easy-going, tail-wagging girl.

Millions of people have written love poems
to their dogs. So, what makes this one special?

Until now, no one has ever written a poem to *you*,
my protector, my Hannah.

We Are Still Ablaze

We came, millions of restless baby boomers,
lifting our promise to a new generation.

Like a fire-sunrise, we exploded with high-sky dreams,
impatient to make our mark and our memories.

How could we know what a half century would unfurl
as we stepped into the mysteries of growing up?

Growing pains bonded us then, but years of joy and loss
bond us now, and we are still ablaze.

mountain palette

spring in the Rockies
lightning thunder rush of ice
world blows sudden-white

> on brilliant green hills
> under diamond rain
> sixty rag-coated elk graze

pink-smash cloud slow moves
sun-gold glaze in windowpanes
early winter dusk

> light-blown icicle
> jagged in steel-cut morning
> melts in blue sunlight

cottonwoods bend-roar
in wind, brave brown leaves hitch
a free blue-sky ride

> snow patches on drab
> hillside grass form continents
> with jagged shores

snow crystal sparklers
dazzle and crash in sun's blaze
rocky mountain joy

> slender black branches
> silhouettes in peach-cool skies.
> night falls in April

portly smug robin
up early to beat the crowd.
take heed, clueless worms

> half pearl in cobalt
> sky, iridescent yellow
> rose-pale aura light

tattered lace edges
melting ice on grey-green lake
encircling grey geese

> surreptitious stars
> slip down handle in darkness
> to swim in big scoop

white blue green ice shards
shatter a tangerine dawn
Evergreen's last frost

> springtime on Squaw Pass
> when bluebirds dance from sapphire
> skies, light on last snow

three black-cloaked old crows
gossip in thin barren trees
spreading their dark lies

> shaggy huddled throng
> rough suede hides dusted with snow
> Genesee bison

tall stately iris
proud purple raving beauty
queen of spring flowers

phosphorescent green
and grape-bruised sky ripped apart
thunder snow drama

                    snowflakes tumble-dive
                  white lacey silver dollars
                      on green-silent grass

steel morning slow mist
forms luminous glass-blown beads
on pine needle spears

                      arrogant magpie
               haughty blue-black white bird-king
                   flaunts new coat feathers

Colorado girl
plows black earth on wind-hewn field
bronzed under noon sun

                    cushions of dense fog
                smother morning with pale gloom
                  chant bleak songs of loss

old gnarled scarred aspen
slowly dying each winter
one branch still buds green

                    bruised violet dawn
                 rising scent of ancient soil
                  hint of first spring rain

trackless sculptured snow
delicate long violet veins
deer tracks mar it first

pristine hillside snow
just one meandering path
of neighbor cat's paws

                              sun-watered droplets
                              linger electric then freeze
                              blue icicle sword

two fat pine grosbeaks
one redhead and one towhead
both eye the plump seed

dark time

In a dark time, the eye begins to see.
Theodore Roethke

Scent of Jasmine

Damascus, haunted city of ancient stories,
fragrant with white jasmine.

Scentless, colorless vapor chokes your hope,
silently slaughters your songs.

Your innocent-eyed children
won't cry for pita again.

Your hidden women
won't wail in silence again.

Your blood-stoked men
won't pray again.

They are safe now
in white winding sheets.

They lie in rows, tightly closed
buds, in the City of Jasmine.

no remorse

one willful ember lies in wait
to catch lonely brush
then stabs wind-chiseled desert crust
drought-cracked and disquieting

with no warning it ignites a holocaust
of unstoppable flame relentless
rushing with no remorse

Abandoned

Oh, Agnes Emma Willie Lizzie Mary
Margaret Johnnie. Babies Eleanor
Tommie. I am abandoning you
without hope.

Fourteen times with child. Hard years.
Lost years except for you precious nine.

I am alone. Cold fear and despair
embrace me now. Still young myself,
but with fractured dreams, I whisper,
where is your charming sugar-talking daddy?

When I knew for sure, I took measures.
Brutal. Nurse-nuns in this cruel town
turned me away, pushed me hard
into this sleet-slashed night.

Gnarled with pain that rips, tightens,
my blood flows unstaunched on tangled sheets,
spreading like brown-edged petals
dropped from spent red roses.

Almost a hundred years have passed…
Feverish, lost, I still float light as thistledown
from this old iron bed.

December

I walk through chill,
white, night's sharp blue.
A windowless palace,
and I can't find solace
or breath.

I can't hear my sigh,
yet I catch its echo.
My steps, melancholy
in a long icy hall, silent.

December's longing
is like none other, lonely,
star-gold, and cold.

Fire Kites

Swarms of red, white, green kites spit fire on winds
of war spiraling from Palestine to Israel, hell on high,
hell below. Incendiary colors signal no compromise,
no peace, no end to carnage. Just a border of hate.

Once upon a time, one sky watched childhood kites
dance with windswept innocence, careless abandon,
joy. Now, both sides seize hate from history's bin.
One people become two, divided under one sky.

Kites dive on hostile winds to twilight. Silk breezes,
cool after brutal sun, fan terrible flames. Sparks arc
in fury—tiny rockets, falling stars—light the darkness
to burnt yellow, the color of yearning.

Fire kites swoop for miles over disputed borders
and ancient stone walls above land once shared.
Coal embers fall, flaming rags ignite ancient forests
and fertile farmlands in an inferno of slaughter.

Fly to the Knife

Let there be no delay in flying to the knife. —Benjamin Rush, Physician
The wound which has lacerated my bosom cannot be healed. —Nabby Adams Smith

Fear buzzes.
Two doctors in church-black
prepare cruel instruments,
rags, hot water. Red coals
grasp an iron spatula, a knife.
A burning cruel knife.
A healing knife.

I must fly to that knife.

Right here in my bedroom,
these strange men
will butcher my breast
and throw it away.

My breast that comforted
the Captain in his despair,
that warmed and nourished
four babes. Now worthless.

Cold sweat now. Shadows
in this dim room smother me.
I fear the knife.

I will not cry out.

Outside, October winds
thrust maple boughs
against the window
to the rhythm of my pulse.
Blood leaves splatter the starched sky.

Two pale surgeons
tie my arms to my chair,
whisper gruesome instructions,
tie a kerchief over my eyes,
unbutton my bodice,
pull my dress from my shoulder,
peel away my petticoat,
loosen the stays in my corset,
slip off my chemise.

Layer by layer,
second by second,
they expose my white breast.
I am ashamed.

Sorrow drenches me,
I touch my breast
and sense the desertion
of God.

The two strangers blur in black.
They lean to me. I brace.
I smell fear in them.
I smell fear in me.

I will not cry out.

I close my eyes behind my kerchief,
Saws, knives, forks, tongs
chime to the beats of my heart,
louder   louder   louder.
I lean to the knife.

I fly to the knife.

I am washed in blood.
I taste red pain.
Exquisite pain.
Silent pain.

I will not cry out.
I will not cry out.

In memory of Nabby, Abigail and John Adams' daughter, who endured a mastectomy without anesthesia in 1811. She did not cry out during the operation. She lived two more years.

word salad

my words mix up again

a rogue tossed salad
nouns once powerful
verbs once alive
adjectives adverbs once vivid
tear mix flip toss spill

even letters and syllables
lately so hard to put together
slice break throw churn
into an *everything but*
the kitchen sink salad

it's all I can serve you
my word salad
a disappointment
when you might have hoped
for a hearty full-course meal

Brown-Eyed Girl

Sha la la la la la la la la la te da...
She was his brown-eyed girl
and she loved him,
or needed to love him,
strong and delicate
as the beating of a bird's wing.

He was the story in her eyes,
light, dusk, night.
She loved him hard,
bore his baggage,
heavy with dark secrets.

He coiled tight, tighter,
finally snapped. He wrecked her,
a restless summer songbird
smashed into a windowpane.

Battered dreams, brutal goodbyes,
wary hellos, taut in-betweens
steeped her in shadows.

She could have cried out
before his darkness bled
into her denial, but instead
she let him scar her.

He lingered way too long.
She showed him out.
His brown-eyed girl.

Hey, where did we go, days when the rains came?
Sha la la la la la la la la la te da...

Inspired by Brown-Eyed Girl by Van Morrison

Nocturne in November

I want to take you with me
down our long straight road
to memory in this Michigan rain,
but the November sky hangs low
and dark and empty. I decide to go alone.

A mighty black storm-hewn tree
cracks in a chaos of branches
and torn twigs, obstructing
my solitude, violating my melancholy.
I can't cry anymore. I just remember.

Cry in Your Rain

Slim, sophisticated, you slip into the waiting room.

Sleek, from your wild raven hair to your black tights
tucked in stylish high-heeled black boots,
you glance around for a seat.

Behind big black sunglasses, you weep, gasp, hiccup
in slender chirps of despair. Almost silent, not quite.

You sit next to me.

Are you hurting? Violated? Newly diagnosed? Abandoned?
Assaulted? Recipient of bad news?

Tears rain from your face, trickle into your arms.
Soak into your black silk shirt.

Let your hot tears rush in a downpour of grief.
Cry in your rain. Let your grief escape in a monsoon.

I wait. I hesitate, and then I lean to you.
May I get you some water—or perhaps a cup of tea?

fallen tree

think calm
until your calm reverberates
in this scan chamber

lie down
lie still in *upward tree pose*
urdhva hastasana

imagine you are a *fallen tree*
stretch body tall, raise arms,
reach, don't breathe

shut your eyes
to the chamber's low sky
closing in on your dreams

breathe
breathe free
fallen tree

At the Twisted Frontier

You always turned the other way
when we walked past the door
to the memory care wing.

Don't ever put me in there, you said.
Now we face that door,
your new home,
your last home.

Only last year you reflected,
your small voice trembling
like a moth fluttering in summer's dusk,
if I could slip now into memory's cruel night,
maybe then, only then, I could forget,
I could escape dementia's murky torment.

Now we open the door. Together,
we face your terrible reality,
your hand grips mine
just as mine gripped yours a lifetime ago.

Daddy, you lingered way too long
at the twisted frontier of knowing
and not knowing.

cancer is a verb

cancer is a wily verb
disguised
as a conniving noun

an active verb
breeding
with undisciplined speed

a tense verb
influencing
past present future

an overbearing verb
controlling
its subject

a moody verb
confounding
doctors and patients

a stalking verb
menacing
killing at random

to be or not to be
isn't that always
the question?

Shut Out

All human things hang
on a slender thread,
the strongest fall
with a sudden crash. —Ovid

You say goodbye
but then follow me
to the elevator.

We stand silent
as its doors
listlessly unzip.

Inside time traps
the moment
self-conscious.

The narrowing doors
are painfully slow
and finally

with only a slender
gash between us
you say I love you.

Don't you know
it is far too late
for all that?

Haibun in the Rain

Spring rain cuts in, out on knives of platinum, teases fuzzy aspen buds, slices pink blossoms. Underneath darkened branches, rain soaks apricot vests of fat fashionable robins taking cover with black and gold caterpillars.

> *reckless blades of rain*
> *slice slash and undress branches*
> *assault early birds*

River of Collateral Damage

People at war with themselves will always
cause collateral damage… —John Mark Green

In America
we count the number of deaths
by shooting. We count the injured.
We count the shooters, the rounds
of ammunition, the 911 calls,
the first responders, the weapons,
the bullets. We count the dead.

We do not count collateral damage.
It's too messy—a blood stain that taints
everyone as it spreads. Nothing changes.

Who can know the reaches of pain?
It's a blood river rushing its arteries
and veins, flooding all in its wake,
forging unforgiving canyons, never
letting up.

Moms, friends, sisters, uncles, sons,
brothers, daughters, dads, aunts,
cousins, coworkers, acquaintances,
teachers, neighbors, caretakers,
even pets—all trapped in the river
gasping in blood of the ones they loved.

healing time

Starship

Every afternoon she floats
from her cradle in a dim vault
to her chartered starship.

Embraced by music
in space-silence and stars,
she blazes with lightning
beamed from an arc
of killing before healing.

A hypnotic Hallelujah!

She journeys in light
from the unknown
to renewal and life.

Every breath she takes
is Hallelujah! Hallelujah!

Hallelujah!

The Surprise of You

Like sun surprises at winter solstice
and scatters light against sky so blue it hurts,
I feel the surprise of you.

I unlock winter riddles
I thought were interred for a lifetime.

My tears run hot, mingle with memories,
and I am washed when you reach for me
after so many years.

One O'Clock News

No respite
until the one o'clock news.

Too late now for good luckers.
Too late for energy senders.
Too late for pray-ers.

It's one o'clock and the doctor is in.
Breaking news flickers on her screen,
ghost images whisper truth
from lopsided apparitions,
my left-over lungs.

Just give me the headline.
I'll wait for the story.

Time to breathe free or new wounds
to scar the light of summer?

So much rests on this news,
the fragrance of solstice,
the yellow of summer,
words still unspoken,
new poems still unraveled.

The news!
Time to breathe free!

When Light Is Right

One geranium petal floats in summer light,
noiseless, elegant, its fire drifts
slow up
slow down
as if in water, buoyant, backlit with radiance.

A spider creates a silken ladder, delicate,
intricate, an almost-invisible lattice,
slow up
slow down
lifting the floating petal.

Together, the petal and the spider plot
a metaphor for her escape from the way
she feels today, rootless, unmoored.

It's a feat only nature or a poem
can summon when light is right,
when she will find her way up.

until further notice

celebrate winter sky
as it brushes new snow

celebrate winter wind
with its melancholy strength

celebrate snow-caps
chiseled behind hillsides

your scan is not until
tomorrow...

until further notice...
celebrate everything

reclamation

this is the year
she will reclaim
her life
she silenced her voice
but she never
abandoned her song
now her song
is fierce and she sings
unbound and wild like a star
raining fire
an arpeggio descending
in a violet night
one voice one spirit
ignited in healing
and might

Six Friends

Seven years old, and early spring daffodils
pop yellow from black-crusted town snow.
It's my birthday, and I am about to check out
my first six library books. My bones buzz.

Six books! Borrowed! Each week! Thousands
of borrowed words. Hours of borrowed wonder.
A week with *Heidi*, *Nancy*, *Jo*, or *Madeline*,
borrowed friends for solace when I escape

to my bedroom, and my old flashlight's arc
warms my comfort cave under heavy quilts,
while in the kitchen Daddy and Mama
breathe fire again.

Transcendence

Time's curtain shuts out pain
thrown on the floor
at the end of the day.
It veils fear and longing
swept and piled in grim corners.

She hollers and heals
behind that curtain.
Thoughts transcend
from chaos to meditation.
Words slip from a crack of light
haunting   brave   lonely.
Poems pound from her dark.

Fragrance of Sliced Limes

Your breeze is silk-cool, and I hide
under the pear-green arms of spring's willow tree.
Supple branches arc and bend from the treetop.

I languish in my leafy tent, tranquil
under a rinsed orange sky etched with twigs
and slender, feather-veined leaves.

You whisper your song of healing,
of renewal, and you refresh my spirit
like the fragrance of sliced limes.

bright spot

back then
she always looked for a bright spot
to offset any dark spot life put in her way
sun gleam striking rain-hammered trees
lone star rising in mourning-cloud skies
dawn bursting through cracks in cobalt rocks

these days
a bright spot means something different
something sinister, a hot shock in technicolor
furious orange and violet
cruel turquoise and sapphire
violent red and pink

today
she won't analyze any bright scan-spots
screaming from a cold screen
or clinical foreboding words:
prognosis biopsy infusion
chemotherapy outcome

tonight
she won't think of the darkest word of all

One Day This Nation

A dirty master in his crude black coat
reeking of white afternoon sweat
bullies a frightened girl to his bed.

A lone woman strides from her dim cabin
to hang her mother's faded quilt, signaling
respite to runaways on the railroad.

A deacon black-robed in righteousness
leaves his prayers, hides in death costumes
to burn and lynch his neighbors.

****

Lincoln's war bends history
 ...with malice toward none...
let us bind up the nation's wounds...

King cries out
I have a dream… let freedom ring...
one day this nation will rise...

Thousands of peace seekers march across
Selma's bridge on Bloody Sunday to searing
fever-violence in summer's white swelter.

North Pier

She meanders through sand and dune grass
to the lighthouse on North Pier,
past wind-slanted fences, past wilted
blue and yellow umbrellas. A crimson sun
ignites heaps of storybook clouds
into slow sparks on her horizon.

She lies on the sunburnt pier under the lighthouse.
Held by dusk's embers, she remembers.
She remembers her first love on North Pier,
lost long ago. Drowsy black breakers
stripe the crimson lake and kiss the pier
with the slow rhythm of soothing darkness.

Swinger of Grapevines

The woods are lovely, dark and deep. —*Robert Frost*

Brush aside dense branches, chase sun
sparking on thick grapevines that run amok
through shadows in the north woods.

Grasp rough bark until it hurts,
kick off the leafy floor, swing, fly,
a wild rhapsody, to the sky.

Sail from yourself through years wasted,
through years anticipated, all the way to light,
all the way to you.

More Light Than Dark

Earth, most of us think
light and dark are equal
at autumn's equinox.

Scientists know light
always triumphs over dark
because you bend sunlight

just enough
to grant us more light
than night.

Earth, enlighten us.

be whole

after darkness, be healed and then be whole
after darkness, be cured and then be well
lift high, seek joy, hold peace within your soul

look up, look skyward, find your aureole
listen, hear gentle heart beats sink and swell
after darkness, be healed and then be whole

rejoice! your shaken self has found a shoal
the storm relinquishes its bitter spell
lift high, seek joy, hold peace within your soul

you bring sweet moments back that darkness stole
your spirit sings, lost in a villanelle
after darkness, be healed and then be whole

this spring's new light promises to console
time to bid last spring's lingering dusk farewell
lift high, seek joy, hold peace within your soul

accept in life crises we can't control
and mysterious fate we can't foretell
after darkness, be healed and then be whole
lift high, seek joy, hold peace within your soul

Destination

May Day morning.
First tender winds.
First time without a sweater.

I hear water music. Spring's waterfall gushes
with the might of a new start. Memory crumbles
like Proust's delicate madeleine, and I remember.
I remember despair in last spring's toxic months,
trapped behind blood walls.

Now I listen to the waterfall's luscious rush
under new buds on slender aspen boughs.

Cruising East Colfax

Cannabis Vacations
Hooked on Colfax
Mile High Men's Club
Good Chemistry
Pleasures at the Park
All in a Dream Comics
Bombshell Tattoo
Green Dragon
Big Hairy Monster
Damselfly
Hush Vapor Lounge
Vaper Jungle
Prohibition
Voodoo Doughnuts
Milkroll Creamery
To the Wind Bistro
Soul Kitchen
Goosetown Tavern
Uber Sausage

Humble Pie Store
Chocolate Lab
Ice Cream Riot
Capitol Cigars
Back in the Game
Machete's Tequila
Mezcal
Lion's Lair
Queen of Sheba
Atomic Cowboy
Thick as Thieves
Bad Kittie Salon
Eye Candy Hair
Bomb Head Shop
Hot Chick a Latte
Romantix
Seven Sins Salon
Revolver: A Salon
End of Days Tattoos

Breathing Time

I steal outside after dusk.
Moonless satin unfolds then enfolds me.
I fade from dark to stars erupting in silence.

Now and then a lone star streaks,
a slender enigma splashes secrets
in timeless galaxies.

I meld with infinity, and in this moment
I do not see behind or ahead—only now,
for this is my breathing time.

time to let go

When it comes, the Landscape listens—
Shadows—hold their breath—
Emily Dickinson

Peeling the Onion

You can peel spike-petals from an artichoke
in anticipation of the reward in its heart,
or you can peel a fresh snappy celery
to marvel at its young pale heart,
you can even peel a tightly-wound lettuce
with its secret whorled crunchy heart,
but a purple onion is best for peeling
if you need a good cry.

Take Me Too

Go ahead, Mother Nature,
take my flowers, this year you win.

You're granting us a long winter,
go ahead, get an early start.

Snow slips from your shoulders.
Take my flowers, all of them.

Winter stalks with unseasonable chills.
Mother Nature, do you always know best?

Have you thought of taking me too?
Take me when the light is low. Take all of me.

Unbound

The sun that brief December day / Rose cheerless over hills of gray,
And, darkly circled, gave at noon / A sadder light than waning moon.
Slow tracing down the thickening sky / Its mute and ominous prophecy,
A portent seeming less than threat, / It sank from sight before it set.
—John Greenleaf Whittier

Snow falls white-hush, windowless,
without solace, without breath.
Blurred and snowbound,
you are alone with no memories.

Your sighs echo silence.
With no portent, you recite a poem
of winter loss you read with your mother
by firelight a lifetime ago.

You remember the *cheerless sun,*
its ominous prophecy. Your words and fears
touch and fall in one rush,
unexpected as your sudden memory.

When winter finally sifts into April,
you sleep forever
free in spring's warmth
unbound.

I Am Done

I fall in hard twilight, surrender,
drift into a storm that roars rings
echoes in my heart and head.

A wild psychic wreck—wheeling
then plunging into bruised swells.
No thought, just sharp shock of ice-fire.

Violent waves wound me, break me.
Where is the cliché of death?
The peace, the light?

Hang on. Let go. Hang on. Let go.
I am down. I am dark.
I am done.

Haughty Dowager

*Celebrating Lake Michigan's North Pier
and Lighthouse in winter*

Ice phantom,
you are a hushed specter
haunting our harbor.
All winter in fog's frozen grip
you watch your white wilderness
sculpted with waves,
motionless and frozen, silent
against your lonely shore.

You are a haughty dowager
in an Edwardian white dress.
Your folds drape in elaborate tucks
and flounces to brush the iced pier
at your feet. You are unyielding,
unsmiling with stifled light.
You stare miles away to a narrow path
of black water resisting winter's hold.

Then on a blue-spring morning
when the air grasps each breath,
and slanted sun-tamed wind chisels
your polished crystal to radiance,
you shed that old dress
and untie your tight corset.

Window Moon

For years, across sky, we talked,
soft moonglow through your windowpane.

He lay in wait, cruel ghoul, he stalked,
he wrought your pain, he watched you wane.

It's too late for gifts of healing,
for we both know your end is nigh.

Death hovers, keeps on stealing,
under your moon we'll say good-bye.

Alas, life won't last forever,
you sigh in your final tune,

forever hold our spirits
in the pale of my window moon.

Funeral Potatoes

No need to cry because I left
with no notice and no overnight bags.
No need to gather with great ceremony
to reflect… laugh… pray… sing…
cry… celebrate or, god forbid, sit…
through a funeral.

In other words, no need to chat about me
when I'm not there to defend myself.

No need to lay out a comfort spread
of funeral potatoes, crockpot meatballs
in simmering sauce, three colors of jello,
green, orange, and jiggling red
with marshmallows and rivers of cool whip
prepared by bustling church ladies in aprons
and sensible shoes who never knew me.

No need to stand around balancing
paper plates with slippery deviled eggs
sprinkled with paprika, tiny cheese squares
stuck with toothpicks flying curly green
and red cellophane flags, or sugar cookies
grabbed at the last minute in the grocery.

No need to wonder why I embraced science
instead of trendy internet remedies—
charcoal, tapping, ice water, juicing, weed,
raw veggies. Hypnosis, aromatherapy,
faith healing. Light therapy, grape seeds, thistles.

No need to whisper stories that judge me
by a chapter of my story
you happened to walk in on.

And, finally, no need to question why I want
my ashes scattered atop Genesee Mountain
under a wildfire sunset where they surely
will blow away with the next cold wind.

And, by the way,
no need to pray for me anymore.

Worried Sky

Worried sky, you are dark and sleepless
with clouds that shift fog-low among blue pines.

Prayers blast from strangers in churches,
full of the righteous, who give no thought
to what is exploding
while she breathes,
while she sleeps,
while she laughs.

Let it be.

Mad cells sicken in a mad concerto.
Roiling clouds hush her greyness,
oblivious to the gridlock of prayers
scratching you, my worried sky.

Let it be.

Mask

Career stared you down,
a pilgrim from the sixties.
You needed a mask to make it
in a good old boys' world.

Transformation complete!
Project on time!
But over budget!
Who knew?

That mask was heavy,
confining, and the price
to maintain it was too high.
Finally, you tore it off and let go.

When You Left

When you left,
I chased you into Third Street.
The meddlesome neighbor
pulled back her sheer curtains.
Tomorrow she will raise the eyebrows
of proper fresh-permed ladies
gossiping in the beauty shop.
My little-girl tears streamed hot,
my head clanged.

I felt myself grow up in that moment,
for it was the first time ever
I let you go.

Our Time

We sit on the floor behind closed doors,
and, in our private language, we bond.

A packed bag waits in my car, ready
for a lone weekend in the mountains,

my time to remember our years
of absolute love. Your head is light in my lap.

I stroke your face and watch your evening eyes
for any sign that we should change our minds.

A fire frees tears that wash us clean.
I breathe the slow rhythm of you.

Every story has an end. I want to end like this.
But who will hold me and wonder if the time is right?

In memory of Sally, my golden retriever, who was with me for a decade.

Eighty-Nine Springs

In iced woods a shadowed cabin
held your unsung dreams.

Snow slashed your first spring,
rain whispered its emerald secrets,
foretelling untilled mysteries.

You tilled a life that yielded plenty.
You sang in rhymes for eighty-nine springs
until peace slipped in gentle as amethyst dusk,
April's gift, and let you rest.

Travelin' Light

It's hard to pack when you have no idea
where you are going or where you will end up.

So, you decide to travel light. It doesn't take long
to rummage through all that came before.

All you pack is hope,
for it can be worn with anything.

You let time loose and cry farewell to your tears.
You won't need them anymore.

Night Passage

Tonight, you sleep gentle, elegant
in your bed for the last time
behind drawn curtains,
black velvet and fringed
with the past.

Beveled mirrors reflect
and bend memories
among a clique of spent perfumes
with crystal stoppers that watch
in the darkness and know.

Dresser sets of inlaid ivory mirrors,
combs, and brushes wound
with long strands of Rita Hayworth hair
wait out the slender night.
Strung out beads cry Hail Mary.

Silver compacts fragrant
with used powder, Lucky Strikes,
half-smoked astride glass ashtrays
spread night sadness among
cherry lipsticks, smeared, worn.

You, restless dreamer,
stir in sleepless sheets,
tossed and wine-stained,
que sera sera
whatever will be will be.

You rise in faded ivory silk,
a shimmery silent night passage.
You rise alone
to lie with decades
of secrets never told.

You Broke the Rules

I like to paint as the bird sings. —*Claude Monet*

Your brush sang on canvas,
vibrated radiance in lavendar sunsets,
sapphire-dappled seas, yellow skies,
haystacks bronzed at noonday.

Under your brush, ponds shimmered
pink-violet, floated delicate waterlilies
fuchsia-white astride lazy green pads
tangled in lush rushes.

You seized moments, impressions,
elusive until you cast your spell of light
on canvas to capture reflections
like exquisite dreams.

Oscar-Claude Monet, audacious, bold,
you broke gloomy rules Old Masters
worshipped for centuries,
and you gave us light.

Letting Go

This is the day I let you go.
I feel the pavement grip
and burn my bare feet.
One hundred fifteen degrees
this harsh August afternoon
under your sun,
white and ruthless.
My body buzzes,
and rings of heat
from your driveway
fuse with my wide-open shock.

Last Business Trip

Your deep red leather attaché case,
slightly battered, but still supple
as the day you bought it, most likely
to celebrate a promotion or a new job,
grows dusty. You don't need it anymore.

Time to let it go. Time to let go
of the high you felt as you fluttered,
a bird from a nest, into a career,
buoyant and ready for all that was new,
facing each morning in a pressed suit
and a pair of power pumps.

That attaché case held reports, pens,
lipstick, toothbrush, Snickers bar,
tattered paperbacks, an extra pair
of pearl earrings in case you left home
with naked ears.

Only you knew how much more you carried
in that case as you ran for flights on high heels,
one heel sometimes broken.

It was heavy with office politics, egos, deadlines,
anxiety. Good old boy dominance. To do lists.
Fighting for a voice. Sleepless hotel nights.
Canceled flights to nowhere, office weekends,
wide-eyed all-nighters.

Now, it's time to take your faithful scarred
red leather attaché case on its last trip—
to the thrift shop where another young woman,
driven, fearless, and on a budget, will fill it
with dreams and baggage she can't do without.

Hair

Hair, hair, hair, hair, hair, hair, hair, flow it,
show it, long as God can grow it, my hair…
—Title song from the musical Hair

Hair. Spikey hair, wild ponytail hair,
singing hair, tangled-in-the-wind
hair, beach-torn hair, think-about-
only-me hair, tame-me-tonight hair,
gardenia hair, strawberry hair,
luscious hair, mahogany-with-gold-
highlights hair, torch music hair,
siren hair, run-your-fingers-through-it
hair, electric hair, messy-bun hair,
diamond-pinned hair, glitter hair,
lush-life hair, French-knotted hair,
pearl-woven hair, hair-kissed hair,
sizzling hair, howling hair, midnight
hair, caress-my-neck hair, entwined-
with-thorns-and-yellow-roses hair,
pull-me-to-you hair, never-let-me-go
hair, aroused hair, screaming hair,
orgasmic hair, oooooh-my-god-hair.
Hair.

The Green Fairy

With sly sophistication
and an aria of anise mystery,
I tempt clever reckless men
as a legend in Europe's Belle Époque.

Wearing nothing but translucent
iced aloofness, my ethereal spirit
enchants countless artists
until they ache with desire.

How I flirt with Wilde
during *the green hour* in elegant bars
until pink tulips dance on his legs
when he staggers into pale mornings.

I entice Picasso and Degas,
and excite the decadence in
their avant-garde imaginations
with my viridescent scent.

As *the green muse*
I lure Baudelaire and Hemingway,
and they lust for my indifference
while they sip *death in the afternoon* cocktails.

Liquid alchemy stirs each lover
in my diaphanous spell as we slip,
hushed, into delicate, beguiling,
and oh-so-pale green Infinity.

With Appreciation

To Carolyn Evans Campbell for inspiring me to write this book and for teaching, mentoring, and supporting me.

To my poetry pals, members of the Evergreen Poets in the Pines, subchapter of the Columbine chapter of the National Federation of State Poetry Societies (NFSPS), for friendship, fun, advice, and encouragement.

To Jean Bell, Carolyn Evans Campbell, and *Barrie Fiedler* for reading my draft, offering great suggestions, and giving me the kick I needed to finish this book.

To Jan Rau and *Sharifa Moore* for advice on cover design.

To Harry Cornelius for taking my photograph.

To Beth Foster Editorial & Design, for finalizing my manuscript for publication.

To Dr. Regina Brown and her oncology team at UCHealth, Lone Tree, for care and healing during the past several years, which gave me hope and time to complete this book.

only time

From the Poet

Throughout my life, poetry has been a journey of joy and comfort. An exploration of solitude. A coming home.

This eclectic collection of poems reflects the mystery of time and how it haunts us. Whether we experience time through the chances we take, pass our time in dreams, or let go of time in a quest for mindfulness, time escorts us from birth to death. Most of us never have enough of it. We seek ways to rush it, deceive it, slow it, deny it, even stop it. Yet, it always eludes us.

I began to write poetry, inspired first in Carolyn Evans Campbell's poetry classes in Evergreen and later in workshops at Lighthouse Writers Workshop in Denver. My poems have won awards at national and state levels and have been published in several anthologies.

I enjoyed a fulfilling full-time career until recently when I reluctantly retired. Now I pursue interests I had put on hold while working and traveling for business.

The Rocky Mountain front range foothills have been my home for more than half my life. Every day, I look to the Continental Divide for solace and inspiration.

only time

www.ingramcontent.com/pod-product-compliance
Lightning Source LLC
LaVergne TN
LVHW041155080426
835511LV00006B/610